Tim McGarry is passionate about interrogating, developing and devising new Australian work. He trained in theatre at the Western Australian Academy of Performing Arts and works as a writer, actor, director and dramaturg. His other writing credits include: Queensland Theatre's sell-out success Trent Dalton's *Boy Swallows Universe*; the Australian Chamber Orchestra's *There's A Sea In My Bedroom*; for the Sydney Opera House *Music for the Dreaming, The Nutcracker* and *Swing Baby Swing*; for Monkey Baa *Thursday's Child, Hitler's Daughter, I Am Jack, Goodbye Jamie Boyd* and *The Peasant Prince – the True Story of Mao's Last Dancer* (all with Eva Di Cesare and Sandra Eldridge); and for Sydney Symphony *Who Needs A Conductor Anyway?* Between 2005–2017 Tim was a Creative Director and Producer at Monkey Baa Theatre Company, one of Australia's largest touring companies for young audiences, where he co-wrote and produced over 20 new Australian works, touring nationally and internationally. His work has been recognised with many awards, including two Helpmanns, two Sydney Theatre Awards and numerous Glug Awards. His modern-day adaptation of *Colleen McCullough's Tim*, will tour widely in 2023 and 2024.

COLLEEN MCCULLOUGH was born in Wellington NSW in 1937. She graduated from the University of Sydney with a bachelor's degree in neurophysiology and in 1958 founded the neurophysiology unit at Sydney's Royal North Shore Hospital and then moved to the Great Ormond Street Hospital in London for four years. From 1967 until 1976 she worked at the Yale School of Medicine in the USA, as a researcher and teacher. It was during this period that she started to write seriously and her first novel *Tim*, published in 1974, received critical acclaim. Her devoted following grew even stronger when her second novel, *The Thorn Birds*, was released in 1977. *Tim* was adapted to the screen in 1979 starring Mel Gibson and Piper Laurie. She wrote eleven more novels and has sold more than 80 million books worldwide, in more than 30 languages. McCullough was named a 'living treasure' by the National Trust of Australia in 1997. In 2006 she was appointed an Officer of the Order of Australia. She died in January 2015 and is without a doubt one of Australia's most revered and loved authors.

Colleen McCullough's

TIM

adapted for the stage by
Tim McGarry

CURRENCY PRESS
The performing arts publisher

christine dunstan

CURRENT THEATRE SERIES

First published in 2023
by Currency Press Pty Ltd,
PO Box 2287, Strawberry Hills, NSW, 2012, Australia
enquiries@currency.com.au
www.currency.com.au

in association with Christine Dunstan Productions

Copyright: *Colleen McCullough's Tim, adapted for the stage by Tim McGarry* ©
Tim McGarry and The Estate of Colleen McCullough, 2023.

Extracts from Margaret Wild's *Fox* and Dub Leffler's *Once There Was A Boy*
have been included with express permission from the works' authors.

COPYING FOR EDUCATIONAL PURPOSES

The Australian *Copyright Act 1968* [Act] allows a maximum of one chapter or 10% of this book, whichever is the greater, to be copied by any educational institution for its educational purposes provided that that educational institution [or the body that administers it] has given a remuneration notice to Copyright Agency [CA] under the Act.

For details of the CA licence for educational institutions contact CA, 12/66 Goulburn Street, Sydney, NSW, 2000; tel: within Australia 1800 066 844 toll free; outside Australia 61 2 9394 7600; fax: 61 2 9394 7601; email: memberservices@copyright.com.au

COPYING FOR OTHER PURPOSES

Except as permitted under the Act, for example a fair dealing for the purposes of study, research, criticism or review, no part of this book may be reproduced, stored in a retrieval system, or transmitted in any form or by any means without prior written permission. All enquiries should be made to the publisher at the address above.

Any performance or public reading of Colleen McCullough's *Tim* is forbidden unless a licence has been received from the author or the author's agent. The purchase of this book in no way gives the purchaser the right to perform the play in public, whether by means of a staged production or a reading. All applications for public performance should be addressed to Lisa Mann Creative Management, PO Box 3145, Redfern, NSW 2016; tel: + 61 2 9387 8207; email: info@lmcm.com.au.

Typeset by Brighton Gray for Currency Press.
Printed by Fineline Print + Copy Services, Revesby, NSW.
Cover features Jeanette Cronin and Ben Goss. Photo by Daniel Boud.

A catalogue record for this book is available from the National Library of Australia

Contents

Notes on the play	vii
Colleen McCullough's Tim	1

Playwright's note

In this rapidly changing, yet often static world for people living with a disability, this work felt ripe for a modern-day theatrical interpretation. I was drawn to the story because I'm attracted to theatre that challenges attitudes, societal norms, morals and ethics. Theatre that can be at times brutal, but personal and ever hopeful. *Tim* does all of that, and more. It's an unconventional story of love, innocence, mortality, vulnerability and prejudice. Its basic premise turns 'the norm' on its head. Older men who seek out younger women are often revered, and receive positive societal affirmations. But can a woman in her 50s partner a man half her age? Society rarely applauds such relationships, and they often become a source of judgement, negative commentary and innuendo.

Tim is about a woman's journey from shame, battling accusations of grooming and seduction, grappling with her own sexual awakening, to a realisation that a full-blown loving union with a much younger man can not only exist, but flourish. It's about a woman who faces her fears and neuroses, and eventually finds clarity and affirmation, allowing her to rise above feelings of inadequacy, and embrace her new-found freedom and truth. Through all of this the young man remains constant. He personifies all that is good in the world, yet is 'imperfect' in the community's eyes. Through him we enjoy innocence, beauty and positivity. He is adventurous and youthful, untarnished by a society hell-bent on prescribing the life he 'should' be leading.

I hope *Tim* helps to shine a light on the many issues facing people with disabilities, their fight for equality, their fight to be recognised as a person first, their disability second.

In the end, whoever we choose to love, however we strive to live a happy life, who are any of us to judge?

Acknowledgements

The journey of transforming *Tim* into a stage production began in November, 2018. The support of the Colleen McCullough Estate has been extraordinary. I'm truly grateful for their trust and faith in the project, particularly the Estate's Chief Executive Bernie Leo, who has been, quite literally, the eyes and ears of Colleen McCullough. I want to acknowledge the following people, some no longer with us, who have enabled me to the best of my ability, to see the world through a different lens: Ruth, Nick, Catherine, Deanne, Ken, Kaylene, Ken, John, Kathy, Kelly, Antun, Richard, Maree, Margie, Brenda, Vanessa, Nola, David, Steven, Stuart, Earl, Craig, Rita, Jane, Danny, Max, Anthony, Belinda, Colin, and so many more. You will never know the depth of my gratitude and respect. Heartfelt gratitude (in no particular order) to Geoff Bartlett, Kate Hood, Vicki Middleton, Kerrie Nothelfer, Clare Dickson, Sue Harding, Craig McMaster, Temnit Teshager, Simon Hinton, Penny Watts, Maria Boyd, Vanessa Wright, Ruth Sweeney, Belinda Maxwell, Lisa Mann, Andrew Crowley and all at LMCM, Jeanette Cronin, Fiona Press, Anthony Phelan, Claudia Ware, Lincoln Younes, Damien Strouthos, Ben Goss, Andrew McFarlane, Valerie Bader, Akkshey Caplash, Julia Robertson, and the entire creative team.

I'm forever grateful to Anne-Marie Heath and The Art House Wyong, together with Peter Ross and The Capitol Tamworth, who commissioned the early drafts and creative development of this work.

To Margaret Wild and Dub Leffler, my deepest thanks to both of you for allowing me to include extracts of your respective works *Fox* and *Once There Was A Boy* in this adaptation.

To producer extraordinaire, Christine Dunstan, who led the charge in bringing this production to the national stage, and director and dramaturg Darren Yap—you are truly two in a million! Thank you.

Tim McGarry

Director's note

When Tim McGarry asked me to collaborate with him on a stage adaptation of Colleen McCullough's *Tim* I knew it was the perfect project for us. We knew it would be a great opportunity to bring *Tim* to life. Not only for the readers who have loved this 1974 book, but to offer *Tim* to a new generation to experience this moving and unconventional love story of Mary Horton and Tim Melville.

I love Tim's writing. He captures the Aussie vernacular perfectly. He has kept the heart of McCullough's novel, but he has found a fresh and gritty danger to this love story of an unlikely couple. The idea of a successful career woman in her 50s and a handsome 25-year-old labourer with a mild intellectual disability becoming a couple is *still* considered taboo in society. We still condemn what we think is not 'normal'. And because of this, I'm very passionate about what *Tim* is about: LOVE IS LOVE. We should try to embrace the differences in people, their cultures and their beliefs.

Over the past few years working alongside Tim, I've loved getting to know our protagonist Mary. She believes she is unloveable and has missed her chance of finding a soul mate. But then Tim comes along and shows Mary that she is beautiful and she is worthy of love. Mary represents that second chances are possible *if* she can open her heart and trust someone else. The tension in the play is will she take the chance to finally 'live a full life and be loved?'

This production wouldn't have been possible without Christine Dunstan leading *Tim* to this world premiere season you are about to witness. My thanks to my creative team: James, Ben, Max, Nigel and Lucy for creating a beautiful design. And finally my respect and thanks to Jeanette, Ben, Andrew, Valerie, Julia and Akkshey who have brought Tim's script and characters to vivid life.

I'm proud to be a small a part of this journey of bringing McCullough's beloved book to the stage.

Darren Yap

Producer's note

I had read an early draft of Tim McGarry's play *Tim* and was captivated by the level of care and thought that had gone into bringing the story into the current day, whilst being faithful to Colleen McCullough's seminal work. Following a week-long creative development in 2020, commissioned by Anne-Marie Heath of the Art House Wyong and Peter Ross of the Capitol Theatre Tamworth, I eagerly yielded and came on board as producer at Draft Two. We went into rehearsal with Draft Eight!

The vision of Tim McGarry, and that of his comrade-in-arms director and dramaturg Darren Yap, have been inspirational to me. These men have lived and breathed this project for three years and finally their brilliance can be experienced by audiences.

I never cease to be enthused and stimulated by creative talent and the team we have assembled for *Tim* is supreme. Jeanette Cronin has been with this project since its early days and we are so fortunate to have maintained her devotion and attracted that of her luminary cast colleagues.

This is a play set in the present day, adapted from a book written 50 years ago, in which many social issues, including prejudice, ageism, and attitudes towards disability are still relevant today. Surely an inditement on our society? I hope *Tim* gives food for thought and goes some way to remedying our bigoted mindset.

Heartfelt thanks to the other Tim, for involving me. It's been a wonderful journey.

Christine Dunstan

Note from the Estate

I consider myself very lucky to have been one of Col McCullough's close mates. Our friendship spanned 35 years. I find it impossible to use her first name. The only thing she hated more than her given name was the saxophone. All her autographs were signed: Col.

I have had this job for six years and to describe it as a labour of love may sound hackneyed but that is what it is.

Col was well established as a neuroscientist at Yale, Connecticut, when she penned her first novel, *Not The Full Quid*, in the early 1970s. Against all the odds it was published. She insisted the Aussie patois remain, as she described it as 'an Aussie book about Aussies'. To her delight, the publishers concurred. However, they said the title had to go. *Not The Full Quid* became *Tim* ... and the rest is history.

It remains an important book, not just in Australia but around the world. Sales have reached almost 30 million, in more than 30 languages. There have been two movies, the first one starring a very young Mel Gibson .

When Tim McGarry first approached me in 2017 wanting to turn *Tim* into a play, both myself and Col's widower, Ric Robinson, were delighted. From day one we have been a hundred percent behind the project.

I was very familiar with Mr McGarry's work, mainly via his brilliant adaptation of Li Cunxin's tale of his younger life *The Peasant Prince* [co-written with Eva Di Cesare and Sandra Eldridge]. With *Tim* in Mr McGarry's hands, what could possibly go wrong? The simple answer to that question is: Not a thing.

He fast-forwarded the story half a century seamlessly and his compassion for the subject matter is clear. The bottom line with the story of *Tim* is that love will find a way, against all the odds.

Tim the play is most certainly the full quid.

Bernie Leo,
Chief Executive,
The Estate of Colleen McCullough

Colleen McCullough's Tim, adapted for the stage by Tim McGarry, was first produced by Christine Dunstan Productions at the Glen Street Theatre in Belrose, Sydney, on 28 July, 2023, with the following cast:

TIM	Ben Goss
HARRY/RON	Andrew McFarlane
MARY	Jeanette Cronin
EMILY/JOY	Valerie Bader
DEE	Julia Robertson
JIM/NATE/RAJ	Akkshey Caplash

Director, Darren Yap
Set Design, James Browne
Costume Design, Lucy M Scott
Lighting Design, Ben Hughes
Sound Design, Max Lambert
Movement Director, Nigel Poulton
Associate Producer, Vanessa Wright, Red Line Productions
Producer, Christine Dunstan Productions

The first production was supported by the Restart Investment to Sustain and Expand (RISE) Fund – an Australian Government initiative.

Australian Government
RISE Fund

The creative development of this play was commissioned and supported by the Art House Wyong and the Capitol Theatre Tamworth.

CHARACTER

TIM, 26-year-old labourer, with a mild disability.
HARRY, Tim's boss.
JIM, a labourer.
MARY, mid-50s Chief Executive of END-CORE Mining.
EMILY, Mary's neighbour and friend.
RON, Tim's father.
DEE, lawyer and Tim's younger sister.
JOY, Tim's mother.
NATE, Dee's boyfriend.
RAJ, team leader of a group home.

SETTING

The action takes place in and around Sydney and the Central Coast of NSW, in the present day.

This play text went to press before the end of rehearsals and may differ from the play as performed.

PROLOGUE

A surreal moment inside TIM's *mind. We see him in a state of anxiety, rocking in anger. He is hearing distorted sounds, truck reversal beeps, men laughing, voices calling for him.*

These noises bleed into the first scene.

SCENE 1

Friday morning. Mary's front yard.

HARRY *appears.*

TIM: I'm sorry. I'm sorry. I'm sorry.
HARRY: Not your fault, mate. Go and calm down.

>As TIM *exits,* JIM *appears.* HARRY *throws the ute keys at him.*

Idiot. You know he can't drive!
JIM: He wanted to give it a go.
HARRY: Bullshit.
>[*Yelling.*] Mrs Parker?

>EMILY *appears.*

EMILY: I saw the whole thing. What in the hell goes through your thick head?
JIM: Sorry.

>JIM *backs away and leaves.*

HARRY: Is your neighbour still home?
EMILY: [*calling out*] Mary.

>MARY *enters, she is heading off to work.*

MARY: [*on her mobile*]—well check it again. I'm on my way. What's happened now?
HARRY: Ute's knocked down the fence—
EMILY: —and flattened the garden.
MARY: For God's sake.
HARRY: I'll replace the palings, and get new shrubs. [*Calling out.*] Tim?

TIM *enters.* MARY *stares at the young workman.*

TIM: Sorry, Harry, the boys told me—
HARRY: It's history, mate, forget it. Can he have access to your yard?
MARY: Of course.
HARRY: Be a good lad and remove the damaged palings, and chuck 'em on the back of the ute.
TIM: Sure.

TIM *doesn't move.*

HARRY: Off you go.

TIM *smiles at* MARY *as he exits.*

It'll be as good as new.

A text message pings on HARRY's *phone.*

Sorry.

HARRY *exits, reading the message.*

MARY: Where in the hell did you find this mob?
EMILY: Back of a Corn Flakes packet. Actually, found them on Google.
MARY: I gather you didn't check the reviews?
EMILY: They were cheap.
MARY: I bet they were.
EMILY: Wanna check out the yard?
MARY: Couldn't bear it. Anyway I'm running late.

As MARY *leaves she collides with* TIM. *After an awkward dance she passes and exits.*

We hear the beginnings of a cicada chorus from the garden.

SCENE 2

Midday.

TIM *is carrying new shrubs from the truck to the rear yard. He is stopped by* JIM, *who is swiping pornography on his mobile.*

JIM: Check out these two going for it. Fuck me, they'd give you a good workout, DT.

TIM *exits.* JIM *continues to watch the pornography.* TIM *re-enters carrying more broken palings from the yard.*

JIM *shows* TIM *the pornography. He drops the palings.*

Well, pick 'em up. [*To himself.*] Slack bastard.

TIM *picks up the palings.*

Chop, chop. Time is money.
TIM: Sorry, Jim.

EMILY *appears, smoking. She observes the workmen.*

JIM: I should think so.

TIM *continues working.*

[*Yelling.*] Don't forget the rest of the plants.
TIM: Which ones?
JIM: [*to himself*] The ones up my arse. [*Yelling.*] On the back of the truck.
TIM: Got it!

JIM *continues swiping pictures.*

JIM: Fuck me.

HARRY *enters.* JIM *looks busy.*

HARRY: Timmy, ask the old girl if I can turn the water off for a minute.
JIM: I will.

JIM *exits.*

EMILY: The old girl says yes.
HARRY: Sorry, didn't see you there.
EMILY: You appear to not see a lot of things.

HARRY *exits.*

TIM: Thanks, Mrs P.
EMILY: Such good manners. You could give those fellas a lesson or two.
TIM: The guys are okay, Mrs P.
EMILY: Guys? I could think of one or two other names for them, pet.

JIM *enters, unaware of* EMILY.

JIM: DT, check out these two going for it.

They both watch the pornography on Jim's iPhone. We hear moaning sounds from the phone.

What I'd give to ride her.
TIM: What do you call that?
JIM: Doggy style, mate, doggy style.

EMILY watches the pornography from behind them.

Wouldn't you like to get your pretty little face between those?

The moaning gets louder.

TIM: Does it hurt?
JIM: You crack me up. Does it look like it hurts?
TIM: A bit.

They keep watching, angling their heads to get a better view.

What's she doing now?
JIM: Spanking his monkey, mate. Spanking his monkey.
TIM: Where's the monkey?
EMILY: Holding the phone.

JIM fumbles to switch off his phone.

JIM: Sorry, Mrs P.
EMILY: Piss off.

JIM disappears. HARRY re-enters, EMILY glares at him, but he makes a wide berth to avoid her. TIM continues to work. We again hear 'orchestra of cicadas' build.

SCENE 3

Friday afternoon. Mary's front yard.

MARY *enters speaking on her mobile.* TIM *is cleaning up the yard and smiles at* MARY.

MARY: Check we've covered regulatory obligations. I can't see the budget ... When? ... Put a bomb under them.

The call ends. TIM *waves at* MARY *as he exits.* EMILY *enters.*

EMILY: Long day?
MARY: Every day's a long day.

EMILY: Favour?

MARY: Sure.

EMILY: Could you grab the garage remote from the boy before he leaves? I've just scored another date on this new app. 'Stick Shift Sixty-Nine'.

MARY: What happened to 'Spicy Meatball'?

EMILY: Dumped.

MARY: Are the builders done?

EMILY: Until the cement falls off the walls.

MARY: Don't tempt fate.

EMILY: Redeemed at the eleventh hour. The yard looks better than ever.

EMILY exits. Finished for the day, TIM *enters with his bag.*

MARY: Where are the others?

TIM: Gone to the pub. Friday afternoon.

MARY: I hear you've done a remarkable job.

TIM smiles.

Back yard.

TIM: Planted new shrubs.

Awkward silence.

Hope they're okay.

MARY: Yes. Good. I'm sure they're terrific. I'll keep them well watered.

TIM: I've just given them a bit of a drink.

Pause.

MARY: Tim, is it?

TIM: Yep.

MARY: Would you like to earn some extra money? The lawn needs a mow and my gardening service has cancelled yet again. Would you be keen?

TIM: Keen?

MARY: To earn some extra money. Cut the grass.

TIM: I have to meet my dad.

MARY: I meant tomorrow or Sunday.

TIM: Sure.

MARY: Great.

TIM: Tomorrow?

MARY: Yes. Or Sunday's fine too.

TIM: Thanks, Mrs—
MARY: Mary.
TIM: Thanks, Mrs Mary.
MARY: Just Mary.
TIM: Dad says I shouldn't call older people by their first name.
MARY: How old do you think I am?
TIM: I don't know. Seventy-five?
MARY: Seventy-five!
TIM: Eighty-five?
MARY: Just Mary. Just Mary.
TIM: Alright. Just Mary.
MARY: Okay. I'll see you tomorrow.
TIM: Okay.
MARY: Good.

>TIM *goes to leave.*

Have you forgotten something? The remote control. For the garage.
TIM: Oh. Here you go.

>TIM *finds the remote in his pocket.*

MARY: Thanks.

>TIM *doesn't leave.*

Off you go. Bye, Tim.
TIM: Bye, Just Mary.

>TIM *waves.* MARY *exits, waving awkwardly back.*

SCENE 4

Pub. Early evening. Same day.

RON *is fixed on a television screen. We hear a greyhound race call.*

RON: Go! Run, Black Panther. Move. Run, ya little bugger! Faster!

>*The race call ends.*

Useless bloody dog.

>TIM *enters as* RON *tears up the betting ticket.*

Can't take a trick today.

TIM: Hi, Dad.
RON: G'day, son. Hot day.
TIM: Yeah. Can I have a beer?
RON: In a tick. Why are you late?
TIM: We finished up a job today. I drove Harry's ute too.
RON: You drove?
TIM: Just in the yard. But I crashed into the old lady's fence.
RON: Jesus God, anybody get hurt?
TIM: Just the fence.
RON: No more driving, son.
TIM: That's what Harry said. I stayed back to clean up because Harry didn't want to 'face the ugly old cow again Monday'.
RON: Were those his exact words?
TIM: Yep.
RON: The other jokers stay back?
TIM: Just me. Can I have a beer, Dad?
RON: Sure.

> TIM *pours a beer and gulps it down.*

Drink it slowly.
TIM: Sorry, Dad.
RON: Where's your pay?

> TIM *hands* RON *an envelope.*

TIM: I got another job too. The lady next door wants me to cut her grass.
RON: What did you say?
TIM: Yes. She's going to pay me. I didn't think you'd mind.
RON: If she's going to pay you, I guess it's okay.
TIM: Can I have another beer, Dad?
RON: In a minute. What's her name?
TIM: Just Mary.
RON: Just Mary?
TIM: Yep.
RON: What's this 'Just Mary' like?
TIM: She's nice.
RON: Does 'Just Mary' have a husband?
TIM: Dunno.
RON: Does she live with anyone?

TIM: Dunno.
RON: You 'dunno' much.
TIM: Nope. Can I have another beer, Dad?
RON: If you drink it slowly.
TIM: I will.
RON: Your mother'll have my guts for garters.
TIM: I will.
RON: Alright, alright.
TIM: Now?
RON: Yes, now. God knows you've earned it.

> TIM *pours himself another beer.*

TIM: Thanks, Dad.
RON: I'll grab another round, and then have one more flutter on the 'diggedy' doggies.

> RON *checks out racing guide as he leaves.*

SCENE 5

The Melville home. Friday night.

TIM *is watching the cricket.* DEE *arrives home. She immediately begins preparing for a night out.*

DEE: TV's a bit loud, Tim. Move back from the screen a little.

> TIM *adjusts slightly, but remains fixated on the cricket.*

Busy day at work?
TIM: I cleaned up Just Mary's yard most of the day.
DEE: Good for you.

> RON *enters.*

RON: Hello, love.
DEE: Hi, Dad.
RON: Your mother's late.
DEE: Probably still at Probus.

> DEE *begins texting.*

TIM: We're gunna thrash the Kiwis. Two for two hundred and thirty-six. We've only lost two wickets.

RON: Don't count your chickens.
DEE: We're well overdue for a win.
TIM: Yep.
RON: How was your day?
DEE: In court for most of it, defending the indefensible.
RON: What's the case?
DEE: Oil and gas giant trying to rape the environment again.
RON: Sounds heavy.
DEE: Defending a company with a staggeringly dodgy moral compass. It's hard to stomach.
RON: It's a job.
DEE: Not the type I was anticipating.
RON: Where are you off to?
DEE: Where all good girls go at the end of a long week. The pub.

   DEE *exits*.

TIM: Can I have another beer, Dad?
RON: I think you've had enough, son. [*Calling to* DEE.] With your artist bloke?
DEE: [*offstage*] You mean Nate.
RON: Yes. Nate.

   DEE *re-enters*.

DEE: Why can't you ever remember his name? It's been six months.
RON: Doesn't seem to wanna stick.

   We hear a text message on Dee's phone.

DEE: Bye, Timbo!
TIM: Can I come?
DEE: A bar full of noisy lawyers. Not your scene.
RON: Stay here and we can watch the rest of the cricket.
TIM: But I want to go.
RON: Settle down, mate.
DEE: How about Sunday, we go to the beach.
TIM: Can we have fish and chips?
DEE: Absolutely.

   DEE *kisses* TIM. JOY *enters, loaded down with shopping bags.*

  Hi, Mum. Bye, Mum. Love you.

JOY: Any more news about Melbourne?
DEE: Not yet.

> DEE *exits.* JOY *is panting, sweating.*

JOY: I swear that hill gets steeper every day.
TIM: We're thrashing the Kiwis, Mum.
JOY: Be a good lad and take that shopping into the kitchen.

> TIM *exits.*

RON: You're late.
JOY: Next time I'll phone ahead and ask permission.

> TIM *enters.*

RON: How was Probus?
JOY: Guest speaker was fascinating.
RON: Who was it?
JOY: Some bloke from The Garvan Institute talking about medical research. Remarkable what they can do nowadays.

> TIM *claps loudly as we hear the crowd roar at the match.*

RON: Settle down, Timmy.
JOY: When did you both get in?
RON: Just after seven.
JOY: I bet dinner was ruined.
RON: Tasted alright to me.
JOY: 'Cause you're full of beer. Did you have a good day at work, love?
TIM: I worked for Just Mary today.
JOY: Who?
RON: Skip it.
JOY: When's this damned cricket finish?
RON: Kiwis are yet to bat.
JOY: We need another telly. Where's Dee gone?
RON: Another date with the 'artiste'.
JOY: Nate.
RON: What kind of art does he do again?
JOY: Painter. I think his speciality is still life.
RON: He could do a self-portrait.
JOY: He dabbles in a bit of sculpture too.

RON: You wouldn't credit it. We get the best-looking kid on the block, can barely count to ten, while the other munchkin wins every university medal and ends up dating a bullshit artist.

JOY: Stop it.

RON: Beats me what she sees in him. He's a bludger.

JOY: For God's sake, just keep your mouth shut.

TIM: Shot! Dad, we're winning!

RON joins in with TIM's enthusiasm.

RON: You little beauty.

SCENE 6

The following day, early Saturday morning. Mary's back yard.

TIM is mowing the lawn. He wears safety earmuffs.

MARY, half-asleep, enters and tries to stop TIM by waving at him.

MARY: Hey. Stop. What are you doing?

TIM waves back. MARY chases after him.

Turn it off! Off!

TIM turns off the mower.

TIM: What's wrong?

MARY: It's seven a.m. That's what's wrong.

TIM: Your lawnmower's a beauty.

MARY: I could care less about the mower, it's too early. Why don't you stop mowing and do some raking?

TIM: Alright.

MARY: The green bin is next to the shed. Do you drink tea?

TIM: Yeah.

MARY: I'll make us a cup of tea.

TIM: Thanks Just Mary.

MARY: Tim. Please. It's not Just… call me Mary. Not Just … call me … only Mary.

TIM: Okay Only Mary.

MARY: Mary, Tim. Mary.

EMILY enters. She has two novels she's returning to MARY.

EMILY: You're up early.
TIM: Morning, Mrs P.
EMILY: Morning, dear.
MARY: Off you go. Be careful of spiders.

>TIM *exits.*

EMILY: Finished them.
MARY: Did you like them?
EMILY: I'm not really into historical fiction. New gardener?
MARY: He did an incredible job yesterday.
EMILY: Were the other lot still here?
MARY: Gone.
EMILY: Lazy bastards. They spend all day taking the piss out of him, then rack off early. He's nothing but a whipping boy. DT, Dim Tim. Spare me.

>TIM *enters.*

MARY: Tea?
EMILY: Tradesmen. Useless all of them. Have you got the remote?
MARY: I'll grab it.

>MARY *exits.* EMILY *watches* TIM *working. He smiles. She smiles back.*

EMILY: Mercy me.

>MARY *enters giving* EMILY *the remote.* TIM *looks at them, laughing to himself.*

MARY: What's so funny, Tim?
TIM: Nothing.

>TIM *keeps working and giggling to himself.*

EMILY: Isn't it sad?
MARY: He seems happy enough.
EMILY: He's a handsome lad.
MARY: I didn't notice.
EMILY: Pull the other one.
MARY: Tim, come and have your cup of tea.
EMILY: What was I saying? Oh yes, tradesmen. All useless.

>TIM *moves to the table for his tea.*

All except you, young man. You are far from useless.

MARY: Em!
EMILY: Late for Pilates.
MARY: Pilates?
EMILY: A body like this doesn't happen all by itself. Besides, I've got another date.
MARY: Not with 'Stick Shift Sixty-Nine' again?
EMILY: No. Hot Rod Seventy-Seven. I'm loving this app.
MARY: Where do you find the energy?
EMILY: I'm old, I'm not dead. Send him over if you run out of chores. I'll keep him busy.
MARY: Goodbye, Emily.

    EMILY *exits*.

Thanks for coming today, Tim.
TIM: No worries.
MARY: Do you come from a big family?
TIM: Nah, just my mum, my dad and my sister.
MARY: Okay. What school did you go to?
TIM: I went to a couple but I didn't finish. I like your hair, Mary.
MARY: Thank you.
TIM: It's got a lot of white bits, like Mum's.
MARY: I suspect I'm not as old as your mother.
TIM: Probably not.
MARY: Tell me, what else do you like to do?
TIM: I like cricket.
MARY: Do you ever go to a match?
TIM: Nope. I get noise sick.

    TIM *finishes his tea.*

I better get back to the mowing.
MARY: Tim, could you come back next Saturday?
TIM: I'll ask Dad.
MARY: Terrific. I'll leave an envelope here on the table with some cash. I'll put my business card in too. Be sure and give it to your dad.
TIM: You're nice.
MARY: Well … thank you.
TIM: You are.
MARY: Okay … well, hop back to work.

TIM *imitates hopping like a rabbit.*

TIM: Did you like that?

MARY *is unsure how to respond.*

It's me being a rabbit.

MARY: Very good. I knew you were a rabbit the minute you started hopping.

TIM *starts the lawnmower, waves to* MARY, *laughing to himself.*

SCENE 7

Pub. Later Saturday evening.

We hear the pub ambience, a race call. RON *returns from the bar with a jug of beer and two glasses.* TIM *is watching the race.*

RON: Come on, you bugger! Run! Run! Give him the whip!

The race call ends. He tears up his ticket.

I cannot win a trick.

TIM: Can I have a beer?

RON: In a minute. How'd it go today?

TIM: Great.

RON: Work hard?

TIM: Yep. Can I have a beer?

RON *pours a beer.* TIM *drinks it in one gulp.*

Can I have another beer, Dad?

RON: Why can't you ever learn to drink it slowly?

TIM: Sorry, I forgot.

RON: So tell me, what's this 'Just Mary' like?

TIM: She's not 'Just Mary' anymore.

RON: What is she now?

TIM: Mary.

RON: Fair enough.

TIM: Her skin is all soft and smooth.

RON: Did she touch you, mate?

TIM: Yes. On the hand.

RON: How old is she?

TIM: I don't know. She's got lots of white hair.
RON: Oh right. Did she pay you?
TIM: Yep and she said her card's inside.
RON: Thanks mate. 'Mary Horton. Bachelor of Economics (Honours)'.
TIM: What's it mean?
RON: It means, son, that Just Mary is a very clever person.

> RON *counts out the money and puts* TIM*'s earnings in his pocket.*

And not short of cash. Two hundred and fifty smackers.
TIM: Can I have another beer, Dad?
RON: In a minute. Did you finish the job?
TIM: No. She wants me to come back next weekend. Is that okay?
RON: The way she pays you can go back every week.
TIM: Can I have another beer please, Dad?
RON: One more beer and I might have one more flutter on the 'geegees'.

> RON *exits.*

SCENE 8

Late Saturday evening at home.

JOY: Why Melbourne?
DEE: I need to get away. I don't know how you've put up with him for so long. You deserve a medal.
JOY: Your father's not that bad.
DEE: He's just so …

> *She can't find the words.*

Anyway, it's not confirmed yet.
JOY: You've only been with this firm, what, ten months?
DEE: It's more than the job, Mum.

> RON *enters, studying the racing guide.*

It's a great opportunity. I'll be working for one of the top environmental lawyers in the country. It just feels … right.
JOY: How long?
DEE: Minimum three-year contract.
JOY: I guess that's the end of Nate.
DEE: He's coming too.

JOY: You've known him less than a year. Where will you live?
RON: Imagine how Tim's gunna react.
DEE: When the time comes, I'll tell him. Where is he?
RON: Out cold. He's exhausted.
JOY: What do we know about this woman? He's very taken with her.
RON: It's keeping him out of mischief.
JOY: Frees you up to skip down to the TAB.
RON: You're not around much yourself these days.
DEE: Stop bickering, you two. Is she paying him properly?
RON: Two hundred and fifty dollars.
DEE: Which you've pocketed until the next race.
RON: No, smartarse.
JOY: How can she afford that?
RON: Well-heeled. How about a cuppa tea, Mum?
DEE: God, she's not your slave, Dad. You know where the kettle is.
RON: It's a bit grim when a man can't ask for a cuppa.
DEE: Honestly. What's her name?
RON: Mary Horton.

>RON *hands* DEE *Mary's business card.*

DEE: Chief Executive, END-CORE Mining. Clearly an 'environmentalist'.
JOY: Look her up on your phone thingy. I'd love to know a bit more about her.
RON: It's like lambs to the slaughter with you, isn't it?

>DEE *researches Mary's name on her mobile.*

DEE: It's called due diligence. 'Horton has extensive experience in running large-scale mining organisations. Prior to END-CORE she was the CEO for the Manx Group.'
RON: No wonder she pays so handsomely.
DEE: Two hundred and fifty dollars. How much of that went on the 'diggedy dogs', Papa?
DEE: She lists her hobbies as 'classical music, reading and she's a self-confessed anthophile'.
RON: Anthophile?
JOY: Something to do with flowers.
DEE: Very clever, Mother. 'Anthophile: A bug or insect attracted to flowers.'
JOY: We should try and meet her.

DEE: Let her know she's being monitored.
RON: Thanks, ASIO.
DEE: I'm going to do a bit more digging on Tim's new bug friend. I smell a rat.
RON: She just wants help in the garden.
DEE: Are you sure that's not all she wants?

SCENE 9

Mary's garden. Mid-February.

Classical music emanates from the house. MARY *directs* TIM *around the garden. He has a pair of shears and carries a large green bag of garden refuse.*

MARY: What on earth did you do to the Japanese maple?
TIM: I trimmed it, like you said.
MARY: More like massacred it.
TIM: You don't like it?
MARY: There's nothing left to like.

    MARY *deflects, when she senses a change in* TIM*'s manner.*

The grevillea could do with a trim.
TIM: You can't trim a grevillea in summer, only winter. Mum said.
MARY: I realise it's summer. And yes, the best time to trim a grevillea is when it's dormant, but I haven't had time. It'll just have to put up with a late pruning.
TIM: Okay.
MARY: Besides, pruning helps control pests and diseases, and it encourages new growth.
TIM: Okay.
MARY: And I might add, the grevillea is dormant. It finished flowering in December. Which is a little later than it normally does, but there you go.
TIM: I said okay.
MARY: Sorry. Yes. You did. Be careful of funnel webs.
TIM: I'm not scared of them.
MARY: You should be. If you get bitten they'll kill you. This has to be the worst year for cicadas. Apparently they can live for years.

> TIM *finds one in the garden. We can hear it buzzing in his hand.*

TIM: I wonder how old this one is?

> MARY *screams and jumps back.*

MARY: Kill it.
TIM: I can't kill it. Where will I put it?
MARY: I don't care. Anywhere. Not near me.
TIM: Do you get cranky a lot?
MARY: Do I sound cranky?
TIM: A bit.

> TIM *keeps working.*

I like your music.
MARY: A Japanese composer. One of my favourites.

I'm glad you appreciate it.
TIM: I guess you don't need me next Saturday.
MARY: Can you weed?
TIM: Yep.
MARY: You could come every Saturday. Help me with the garden. Mow the lawn, trim the trees.
TIM: Okay.
MARY: I'll pay you.
TIM: I said okay.
MARY: Good.

> *Awkward silence.*

You better get back to work.
TIM: Sure.
MARY: Tim.
TIM: What?
MARY: I'll try to be less … cranky from now on.
TIM: Good.

> TIM *keeps working. He sees* MARY *watching him. He does a 'bunny hop'. She laughs.*
>
> *He exits.*

SCENE 10

Six weeks later. Early Tuesday morning at Ron and Joy's house.

RADIO ANNOUNCER: [*voice-over*] It's just gone eight a.m. on this glorious autumn day. Here's an old tune that will bring back the seventies for listeners.

    RON *is on the phone to* MARY. JOY *is playing Sudoku.*

MARY: Ron, it's Mary. Tim's Saturday friend.
RON: Hello, Mary.
MARY: Sorry to phone so early.

    JOY *listens into the call.*

RON: We're always up with the birds. How's Tim going?
MARY: He's been a lifesaver.
RON: Not needed next Saturday?
MARY: He is and he isn't. I have a weekender on the Hawkesbury. Would it be okay for him to come up and help me out?
RON: I'll just put you on speaker.
JOY: Mary, it's Joy.
MARY: Hello, Joy.
JOY: You mean overnight?
MARY: Is that okay?
RON: A change of scenery will do him a world of good.
MARY: The weather will be a bit cool.
JOY: He doesn't feel the cold.
MARY: Can he swim?
JOY: Like a fish.
RON: We'll make sure he gets to you bright and early.
MARY: I'll swing by and pick him up.
JOY: We'll just need to check with Tim, though.
MARY: Of course. Is there anything I should know?
JOY: He can get carsick.
RON: Keep the windows down. Otherwise, he's as fit as a fiddle.
JOY: Rarely needs a Panadol.
MARY: Half his luck. I'll see you Saturday.

RON: Cheerio.
JOY: Bye, bye.

Call ends.

RON: What's the matter?

JOY *shakes her head.* DEE *enters.*

DEE: Who was that?
JOY: The mysterious Mary Horton.
DEE: So, how is the bug lady?
JOY: Very well spoken.
DEE: What did she want?
RON: She's got a place on the Hawkesbury. She wants Tim to lend a hand up there next weekend.
DEE: Lend a hand?
JOY: She wants him to stay away. Overnight.
DEE: You said no I hope.
JOY: I said we'd check with Tim.
DEE: We've never actually met this woman.
JOY: No. We have not.
RON: Settle down. It's been over a month.
DEE: You are beyond belief.
JOY: I guess it can't hurt.

TIM *appears, getting ready for work.*

TIM: This shoe's got a knot.

RON *takes the shoe and undoes the knot while* TIM *puts on the other shoe and waits.*

RON: Now listen, Tim, that was Mary on the phone.
TIM: I want to go. She already told me.
RON: If you're keen, that's fine by us.
JOY: Is she as nice as she sounds, love?
TIM: Yep.
JOY: Will you be okay staying overnight?
DEE: Tim. This lady. Is she … friendly?
TIM: Yep, really friendly.
RON: Still in court?
DEE: Yes.

JOY *hands him his lunchbox.*

JOY: There you go, love.
RON: And one shoe unknotted.
TIM: Thanks.
DEE: I'm late, but we're not finished discussing this whole 'bug' thing.

> *As* DEE *rushes out the door, we hear the distinct horn of Harry's truck.*

Tim, Harry's out front.

TIM: Bye.
JOY: Laces?
TIM: I'll do it in the truck.

> TIM *exits.*

JOY: I'm not going to sleep a wink all weekend.

SCENE 11

Mary's cottage, the following Saturday.

TIM: Wow, is that the Hawkesbury?
MARY: Quite a view, isn't it.
TIM: Beautiful.
MARY: You did well in the car.
TIM: I want to get my driver's licence one day.
MARY: To drive a car?
TIM: Yep, Mum said. One day.
MARY: Right.
TIM: Is that an island?
MARY: Lion Island.
TIM: It's a weird shape.
MARY: It was originally named Mount Elliott Island. After the Governor of Gibraltar, because it was said to resemble Gibraltar. I'm a bit of a local history buff.

> *Beat.*

Too much information I suspect.

TIM: Why don't you live here all the time?
MARY: Work. I've got vague memories of living here when I was younger.

TIM: Are your mum and dad here?
MARY: No. I lost my parents when I was six.
TIM: Did you find them?
MARY: No. I meant they died. I grew up in an orphanage.

> TIM *stares at the view.*

Mesmerising, isn't it? Do you want to grab your bag from the car?

> *As* TIM *exits,* MARY *receives a text message.* TIM *returns with his overnight bag.*

Work never stops. I might be a bit daring and switch it off for the weekend.
TIM: Can we go for a swim?
MARY: Sure, why don't you change into your swimmers and we'll go down to the inlet.

> TIM *exits.*

[*Yelling off.*] Did you pack a hat?
TIM: Yep.
MARY: Do you need a towel?
TIM: Nope.
MARY: I have some sunscreen in my bag.

> TIM *appears in his swimmers and has a towel draped over his shoulder.*

Let's go.
TIM: You said we were going swimming.
MARY: You can swim to your heart's content. I never go into the water.
TIM: No.
MARY: I'll watch you.
TIM: I don't need watching.
MARY: I didn't mean that.
TIM: I don't want to swim by myself.
MARY: It's getting a bit cool.
TIM: I want to swim with you.
MARY: I don't have any swimmers.

> TIM *is agitated.*

TIM: No.

MARY: What's wrong?
TIM: No. No. No.
MARY: Tell me.
TIM: You don't want to swim.
MARY: I told you—
TIM: You don't want to swim with me.
MARY: That's not true.

> TIM*'s anxiety is increasing.*

TIM: No. No. No.
MARY: I just never go in.
TIM: You don't want to swim with me.
MARY: Not at all, I just don't like my legs.
TIM: There's nothing wrong with your legs.
MARY: It's just—
TIM: You don't like me.
MARY: No, that's not true at all. I could go inside and see what I can find.
TIM: Go.
MARY: Here, put some sunscreen on.

> MARY *exits.*

[*Offstage.*] But I can't really swim … I can barely dog paddle.
TIM: Everyone can swim.
MARY: Not everyone. You'll have to look after me when I'm in the water.
No playing tricks on me.
TIM: Come on.
MARY: No dunking me.
TIM: Okay.
MARY: Or disappearing on me.
TIM: Hurry.

> TIM *can hardly contain his excitement.*

MARY: Do you promise?
TIM: Okay.
MARY: Sure?
TIM: Come on.

MARY: I'm coming.
TIM: Hurry up.

> MARY *enters. She's torn the sleeves off a shirt, turning it into a midriff, and has cut down long pants into shorts.*

MARY: Ready.
TIM: Great. Now we can both go swimming.
MARY: Can't wait.

> TIM *grabs her hand and they run down to the beach.*

TIM: Come on, Mary.

SCENE 12

The Melville home. Saturday evening. Late April.

RON *and* JOY *are watching the television.* NATE *is pacing, waiting for* DEE.

NATE: Dee, we're late. I don't want to miss the speeches.
DEE: [*offstage*] Two minutes.
JOY: Where are you off to, Nate?
NATE: A friend is launching a new exhibition down at the MCA tonight. I've been itching to see it. Looks really cool.

> DEE *enters reading from her iPhone.*

DEE: 'An unnamed senator was arrested after leaking secret information about Australian mining company END-CORE.'
RON: You're like a dog with a bone.
JOY: Shoosh, both of you.
DEE: This article isn't exactly painting the executives of End Core as model citizens.
RON: You're not in court now.
DEE: Don't patronise me. She's got no Facebook, no LinkedIn, no Twitter.
NATE: No social media?
DEE: It's just odd.
RON: It's not a crime to want privacy.
DEE: At the very least you should meet her.
RON: I already have, smart aleck.

DEE: God, you're rude. When?
RON: This morning, when she picked him up.
DEE: Tim's not the only one being groomed.
RON: For the love of God, what's all this got to do with her needing a gardener?
DEE: She could've hired anyone. Why hire Tim?
RON: Because he's a bloody good gardener.
JOY: I can't hear the telly.
NATE: Has anyone asked Tim what he thinks?
DEE: He can't articulate what's going on.
JOY: He's not stupid.
DEE: I'm not saying he's stupid.
NATE: I'd be happy to take him down the pub for a beer. You know, have a chat. 'Sus' out what's going on.
DEE: We should be talking to her not Tim.
NATE: Just a thought.
DEE: When's he coming home? I need to talk to him.
RON: Late Sunday afternoon.
JOY: What about?
DEE: Melbourne's confirmed.
JOY: Congratulations, love, that's wonderful news.
DEE: Thanks, Mum.
RON: Good for you.
JOY: Do you want me to talk to him?
DEE: He needs to hear it from me.
JOY: When do you start?
DEE: We're heading down in about six weeks.
RON: We?
DEE: Nate's coming too.
RON: [*under his breath*] God almighty.
JOY: Are you looking forward to the move, Nate?
NATE: I'm stoked. It's going to be mind-blowing. Great for Dee's career too.
RON: Will you attempt to find work in Melbourne, Nate?
NATE: Yes, Ron. I've got a cousin who runs a gallery in South Yarra. She's going to introduce me to a few curators.
RON: Curators?

JOY: Ron, can you empty the bin?
NATE: Yes. Curators, Ron.

> RON *doesn't move, just stares at* NATE, *who clocks* RON's *coldness.*

I want to get an exhibition up, once we've settled in.
RON: Shame we've never see any of your … art, Nate.
NATE: Yes it is, Ron.
DEE: Nate's an incredible artist.
RON: I bet he is.
JOY: Ron. Bin.
NATE: Let's go Dee.
DEE: As well as being modest. He was shortlisted for the national still-life award.
NATE: Dee.
JOY: An award.
RON: Still life?
NATE: Yes, Ron.
JOY: That's very impressive. Would you like to come and speak at Probus?

SCENE 13

The beach later that night.

TIM *is sitting under the moonlight by the fire. Classical music emanates from the cottage.* MARY *enters with a hot chocolate and a glass of red wine.*

MARY: One hot chocolate.
TIM: Thanks, Mary.
MARY: Can you hear that train in the distance?
TIM: Just.
MARY: Sydney to Newcastle. It always reminds me that civilisation is not too far away.

> *They sit in silence.*

You really like swimming.
TIM: I love it.

MARY: Didn't think you'd ever come out. Sorry I couldn't stay in longer. The water's getting a little too cold for my liking.

> TIM *reaches out and touches* MARY*'s hair. She recoils.*

Uh. I thought it was a bug in my hair.

TIM: Sorry, I just wanted to touch your hair. Did I scare you?

MARY: No. Not at all.

TIM: I like you.

MARY: I like you too.

TIM: I like your music too.

MARY: It helps me relax. What kind of music do you like?

TIM: What kinds are there?

MARY: Lots. This is one of my favourite pieces. Chopin.

TIM: Can I ask you something?

MARY: Sure.

TIM: What's an orphanage?

MARY: It's a place you live when you don't have a family.

TIM: Did you like it?

MARY: It was okay. I felt safe.

> *They sit for a while listening to the music.*

It's getting late.

TIM: I might turn in.

MARY: Okay.

> TIM *gently kisses her forehead.*

Night, Tim.

> *He goes to leave.*

TIM: I like talking to you, Mary.

> *He exits.*

MARY: I like talking to you too.

> *We see* MARY, *deep in thought, contemplating Tim's gentle kiss. She finishes her wine and exits.*

SCENE 14

The Melville home. The next day.

JOY *is unpacking Tim's overnight bag.* RON *is on the phone.*

RON: That sounds terrific, but only if he pays his own way—
JOY: Put these in your dirty-clothes basket. Good man.

> TIM *takes clothes to his room.*

RON: Thanks, Mary. Have a good trip … Cheerio.

> *As* RON *finishes the phone call,* DEE *and* NATE *enter.*

DEE: Did I just see the elusive mining maggot nattering on her mobile?
RON: I think the word you're looking for is magnate … And she was 'nattering' to me.
NATE: She's got a flashy bloody car.
DEE: Strange how she never comes in.
JOY: Why'd she call?
RON: She's going away for a few weeks. Some mining conference.
JOY: What was that about Tim paying his own way?
RON: She wants to take him on a trip.
JOY: When? Where to?
RON: Later in the year. Up north. The Daintree I think.
DEE: On a plane? Tim will have a fit.
JOY: I'm not sure a flight is such a good idea.
RON: Relax. God almighty, nothing's set in stone.
JOY: Sounds like you've already given her the go-ahead.

> TIM *enters from his room.*

Did you have a good weekend, love?
TIM: Yep, we cleaned up the gardens and next time we're gunna build a barbeque.
NATE: How you going, mate?
TIM: Hi, Nate.

> JOY *continues to clean out Tim's bag and holds up a picture book,* Once There Was a Boy *by Dub Leffler.*

JOY: Is this yours?

TIM: Yes, Mary's teaching me to read.
RON: Can you read it?
TIM: A bit.
JOY: Could you read a bit for me?

>   TIM *reads slowly.* NATE *turns the television off.*

TIM: 'Once, there was a boy who lived on an—'
JOY: Island.
TIM: —island. He lived there all by him—'
JOY: Himself.
TIM: '…himself.'
JOY: Keep going.
TIM: 'He lived in an—'
JOY: Ancient.
TIM: '—ancient boat that was made from an … '
JOY: Ancient—
TIM: '—ancient tree … One day he looked down on the beach and saw something moving. Closer and closer and closer…'
JOY: Someone.
TIM: '…Someone else! Here, on the island!'

>   *They are stunned by Tim's ability to read. Speechless.*

NATE: Wow, that's pretty impressive, mate.
TIM: Thanks.

>   *Pause.*

JOY: And Mary's been teaching you?
TIM: Yeah.
RON: That's incredible, son.
TIM: Thanks, Dad.
JOY: Do you want to keep your book in your room?
TIM: Yes, thanks, Mum.

>   TIM *exits, taking the picture book and his overnight bag.*

RON: What do you have to say for yourself now, smarty pants?

>   DEE *remains silent.*

All this garbage running around in your head. Well that disproves your bullshit argument.

DEE: Disproves nothing.

> TIM *re-enters.*

JOY: Are you tired, love?
TIM: Yes, I'm going to bed.
RON: Sweet dreams.
NATE: Night, mate.
DEE: Love you.
TIM: Love you, too.
JOY: I'll come and tuck you in.
TIM: I don't need tucking in, Mum.

> TIM *exits.*

RON: Wanna check to see if Mary's hiding under his bed?

> RON *laughs.* DEE *glares at him.*

SCENE 15

Mary's cottage. Four weeks later.

TIM *drags* MARY *into the garden. Classical music emanates from the cottage.*

TIM: Look. It's flowering. It's all flowering.
MARY: It's magnificent. Wow, what a gardener you are!
TIM: You've been away for too long.
MARY: A couple of weeks? Did you miss me?
TIM: I did. Dad said I was a bloody nuisance.
MARY: It was great you got to spend time with Dee before she leaves.
TIM: She wants me to visit her. Will you come?
MARY: To Melbourne? We'll see.
TIM: Mum got me a new book. Can we keep reading it?
MARY: Sure.

> TIM *heads in to get his book and returns with Margaret Wild's* Fox.

'*Fox.*'
TIM: You start.
MARY: No, you start.

TIM: 'With Magpie clinging to his back, he races through the scrub, past the—'
MARY: Stringybarks—
TIM: '—stringybarks, past the clumps of yellow trees—'
MARY: '—and into the blueness. He runs so swiftly, it's almost as if he were flying.'
TIM: 'Magpie feels the wind streaming through her feathers and she—'
MARY: '—rejoices.'
TIM: 'Fly, Dog, Fly! I will be your missing eye, and you will be my wings.'

TIM closes the book.

Thanks, Mary.
MARY: For what?
TIM: Acting like I'm normal.
MARY: You are normal.
TIM: No I'm not.
MARY: Well, I think you are.
TIM: I know I'm not.

TIM plays with her hair again. MARY *abruptly gets up.*

MARY: I'm just going for a walk, Tim. I'll be back soon.

MARY walks out into the garden. TIM *continues to read.*

She drops to her knees. Grief-stricken, weeps. TIM *appears.*

TIM: Mary, are you okay?
MARY: I'm fine.
TIM: Do you feel sick?
MARY: No. I just needed some air.
TIM: Sure?
MARY: I'm alright. Truly, I am.

She tries to stand.

No need to worry about me. Do you believe me?
TIM: I believe you.
MARY: Thanks, Tim. I didn't realise how nice it was to be looked after.
TIM: I'll always look after you.
MARY: I'll never need to worry while I've got you around.

TIM: Never.

He leans in, hugs her and gently kisses her on her forehead.

MARY: Better get some sleep. We might head off early in the morning.

TIM: Okay.

MARY: I might just stay out here for a bit.

TIM *exits.*

MARY *is alone and overwhelmed by a sense of love and confusion.*

We hear Gounod's 'Ave Maria'. It continues throughout the following scene.

SCENE 16

The Melville home. Friday night. Late June.

JOY *is returning home with shopping.*

She moves slowly through the house, measuring her breathing as if fending off bouts of chest pain. She pants through the pain. She is distressed and hot, wiping her forehead with her handkerchief. She slowly walks towards a chair. As she sits, she half-smiles, but is once again wracked by pain. The pain under her left shoulder blade begins to become more intense, and she grips her arm, hoping to relieve the discomfort.

At times she is panting for breath as if fighting off some huge, maddening beast. She leans forward in the chair, her arms folded across her chest, her fists digging into her armpits. She is in agony. Small, moaning whimpers escape her mouth each time the pain engulfs her chest.

After what feels like an eternity the pain seems to lessen, and JOY *begins to lose consciousness.*

The lights fade as if night has fallen.

SCENE 17

The Melville home. Late June.

It's just after 7 p.m. RON *and* TIM *walk through the door to find the house oddly quiet.*

RON: Hello. Where's Mum?

RON *turns on the lights.*

Joy?

TIM *steps further into the house, sees* JOY *slumped.*

TIM: Mum.

RON: Joy?

She doesn't respond.

Tim, stay with Mum. I'm going to call an ambulance.

RON *exits.* TIM *gently holds his mother's hand.*

TIM: Wake up, Mum. Are you feeling sick? Mum?

JOY *starts to murmur. She is semiconscious.*

JOY: Tim?

TIM: I'm here, Mum.

RON *re-enters.*

RON: The ambulance is on its way.

JOY: Christ … Ron … the pain … awful.

RON: Try and stay calm.

JOY: I've wet myself.

RON: What's the odd leak between friends.

JOY: The chair's wet.

RON: It'll dry out.

TIM: Mum.

RON: Listen, mate, could you wait out on the street for the ambulance?

TIM *walks out, unable to keep his eyes off his mother.*

JOY: What'll happen to Tim?

RON: Everything'll be okay, Joy. No need to worry, love.

JOY: Can't leave … Tim … all alone.

RON: You're not going anywhere. Stay with me.

JOY: You need to—

JOY *is overcome with pain again.*

RON: Hang on, love.

JOY: No, listen to me—

RON: Please. Hang on.

JOY: —You need to—

RON: I'm here.
JOY: Make sure—Tim—

> JOY *is struck by another massive pain in her chest. She has lost her fight.*

RON: Joy. Stay with me. Joy?

> RON *weeps. We hear the ambulance in the distance. It is too late.*
> TIM *enters.*

SCENE 18

The Melville home. Late Saturday night.

The room is different. The cushion from the couch has been removed.

RON: All the funeral arrangements? He won't cope—
DEE: He will.
RON: It's the best thing for him.
NATE: It's hard to comprehend.
RON: Why didn't I come straight home?
NATE: She wouldn't want you to blame yourself.

> TIM *enters.*

RON: How's my little mate?
TIM: Is she really truly dead?
RON: Yes, mate. She's really truly dead. Do you want me to make you a sandwich?
TIM: Okay.

> RON *and* TIM *exit.*

DEE: Why didn't he come straight home?
NATE: You can't put that on your dad.

> *We hear the doorbell.* NATE *exits.*

MARY: [*offstage*] Hi. I'm Mary.
NATE: [*offstage*] Nate. Please, come in.

> *They enter.*

  Dee, this is Mary.
DEE: Sorry?

NATE: Tim's friend. Mary.

    DEE *tries to hide her surprise.*

DEE: Oh.
MARY: I'm sorry for your loss.
DEE: Thank you.
MARY: How's Tim?
DEE: He's okay.
MARY: A terrible shock.
NATE: Yes.

    An awkward silence.

MARY: I guess this'll slow down plans?
DEE: Plans?
MARY: Melbourne.
DEE: Melbourne?
MARY: Tim mentioned it.
DEE: Did he?

    RON *appears.*

RON: Mary.
MARY: Ron, I'm so sorry. This is a dreadful loss for you all.
RON: Dreadful. Can we offer you a cuppa tea?
MARY: No thanks. I won't stay. How's Tim?
RON: Dazed. I'm sorry to bring you into all of this. It's all a bit much, autopsies, undertakers, the burial. Tim simply won't cope—
DEE: He'll cope.
RON: I don't want to leave him by himself.
DEE: He'll just come with us.
MARY: I'm glad I can be of help. I could bring him back for the actual service if you like?
DEE: Yes.
RON: No. Too many people. Best if he stays away.
MARY: Whatever you think.
RON: I'll help him pack a bag.

    RON *exits.*

DEE: What the actual fuck are you doing here?
MARY: Your dad asked me to take Tim.

DEE: Where? Take him where?
MARY: Up the coast—
DEE: He needs to stay here.
NATE: I think Ron's made up his mind.
DEE: I don't care.
NATE: Dee—
DEE: I don't care what Dad thinks. How does Tim ever get a chance to say goodbye.
MARY: I tend to—
NATE: Has anyone actually asked Tim?

> RON *and* TIM *return.* TIM *carries an overnight bag.*

TIM: Mary.
MARY: I'm so sorry about your mum, Tim.
DEE: Dad, Tim should stay with us.
RON: There is only so much the boy can take.
DEE: But—
RON: —It's settled. Enough.
DEE: For Christ's sake, Dad.
RON: I said enough.

> TIM *covers his ears.*

DEE: I just can't believe you'd offload him at a time like this.
RON: I'm doing what's best for him.

> TIM *begins to get agitated.*

DEE: Are you completely fucking blind?
TIM: Stop.
DEE: Doesn't internet dating work for you?
MARY: I'm not—
DEE: Convince me that's not what's going on.
MARY: I'm old enough—
DEE: —to be his mother? You're telling me.
RON: Cut it out.
TIM: Quiet.
DEE: It's all too pathetic for words.
MARY: If you're suggesting—
DEE: I'm not suggesting it. I'm saying it straight out.

TIM *begins to hit himself.* DEE *goes to* TIM *and talks him down.*

It's okay, mate. I'm sorry I got too loud. It's okay. It's okay. Just breathe with me. That's it.

TIM *begins to calm down.*

TIM: No more yelling.
DEE: No more yelling. I'm sorry. It was my fault.
TIM: You're too loud.
DEE: I know. We shouldn't have raised our voices. I'm sorry. I'll get you some water.

DEE *exits.*

MARY: I'm sorry if that's what you all thought—
NATE: What did you expect us to think?
MARY: I had no idea—
NATE: It didn't cross your mind?
MARY: No. Never.

DEE *returns with the water.*

NATE: You must've had an inkling.
RON: Give it a rest.
MARY: I should go.
TIM: Can I still go too?
RON: Sure, mate. Mary, I'm sorry.
MARY: It's okay.
RON: Please accept my apologies.
MARY: After the funeral I'd love you to come up to the cottage.
RON: I might take you up on that offer.
TIM: Bye, Dad.
RON: Be good, son.

DEE *hugs* TIM.

DEE: I love you.
TIM: Love you too.

MARY *and* TIM *exit.*

RON: You're an absolute disgrace.
NATE: I thought she was supposed to be old.

DEE: I didn't buy any of that. She's been working on him from the minute she met him.
RON: Rot.
DEE: But you wouldn't hear a word against her. You've just had your eyes on the cash.

RON *is silent.*

Where's all his money gone? On the horses or on the dogs?

RON *maintains his silence.*

NATE: Ron, you've gotta admit, she's pretty cagey.
RON: Jesus, you're a piece of work, mate.
DEE: Leave Nate out of it.
RON: Piss weak.
DEE: Dad.
RON: I should've known you didn't come up with all this shit by yourself.
DEE: Dad, leave it.
RON: It was you, wasn't it?
DEE: Dad.
NATE: Dee has a perfectly valid concern. Tim's—
RON: You're the one who's filled her mind with all this filth.
NATE: All I'm saying is—
RON: When are you going to drop this idiot?
DEE: Dad.
RON: You're full of shit. Pissing in the wind.
DEE: Stop it.
RON: I oughta deck you, you arsehole—

RON *moves towards* NATE.

NATE: You're fuckin' insane, mate.
DEE: Dad!

SCENE 19

Mary's home. Later that night.

MARY: She was vile. Outright accused me of seducing him.
EMILY: Was Tim in earshot?
MARY: He heard everything. Every word.

EMILY: I would've poked her eyes out.
MARY: Not my style, I'm afraid. I was too stunned.
EMILY: How is he?
MARY: Totally and utterly confused I suspect.
EMILY: Did he say anything in the car?
MARY: Not a word. Silent the entire way home.
EMILY: Poor bugger.
MARY: I'm amazed he can sleep.
EMILY: Are you going to the funeral?
MARY: No.
EMILY: Wise move.
MARY: Neither is Tim.
EMILY: What? Not going to his own mother's funeral? Really?
MARY: We're heading up the coast in the morning.
EMILY: I'm sorry but that's not right.
MARY: Ron doesn't think Tim will cope.
EMILY: Maybe Ron's the one who won't cope. It's the boy's mother.
MARY: But it's Ron's decision.
EMILY: No, it's Tim's decision.
MARY: Ron was adamant. Immovable on the subject.
EMILY: They can't just wrap him up in cotton wool his entire life.
MARY: I agree.
EMILY: Mary, can I be frank?
MARY: Sure.
EMILY: What happens when Ron goes?
MARY: That could be years away.
EMILY: You're not going to like hearing this but maybe now's the time to pull up stumps.
MARY: I can't do that to him.
EMILY: Life's full of disappointments. He'll survive without you.
MARY: I honestly don't know.
EMILY: The question is, will you survive?
MARY: Of course I will.
EMILY: Really? Sorry to be blunt, but I think you're in too deep with this family.
MARY: I just … I never thought I'd ever care this much about anyone.
EMILY: You're not his mother.

MARY: No. I'm not.
EMILY: But he could very easily see you in that role. Particularly now.
MARY: I can't desert him.
EMILY: No. I don't think you can.

SCENE 20

Mary's cottage. Evening. Three days later.

TIM *sits out by the fire.* MARY *brings him a beer and a wine for herself.*

MARY: Another beer?

> TIM *doesn't respond. They sit looking at the fire.*

TIM: What's dead mean?
MARY: Sorry?
TIM: Dead. What does it mean?

> MARY *takes* TIM's *hand and places it near his heart.*

MARY: Well, can you feel your heart beating in your chest?
TIM: Yes.
MARY: While it beats we're alive. But when it stops, we stop. It means we're not alive anymore. That's what being dead is. It's a bit like going to sleep forever.
TIM: So Mum's gone to sleep. Forever?
MARY: Yes. She's in the ground under a blanket of grass.

> TIM *nestles into* MARY. *She slowly draws away.*

You know, life's made up of meeting many people, liking some, loving others, but then for many reasons they leave. Leaving is the hardest part, especially if you love them.
TIM: Does that mean one day you'll die, too?
MARY: One day we'll all die, but not for a long time.
TIM: I want to live forever.
MARY: Come on, let's head inside. It's getting cold.

> MARY *and* TIM *begin to clean up glasses and chairs and* TIM *puts the fire out.*

TIM: Mary, when you hugged me. What was that called?
MARY: I don't know. It's called comforting, I guess.

TIM: I like it.
MARY: Did it help you feel better?
TIM: Yep. I'd like you to comfort me every day.
MARY: Forget it. It ain't gunna happen, sunshine.
TIM: Can I ask you something else?
MARY: Sure.
TIM: Why was Dee so angry?
MARY: She was upset about your mum.
TIM: Are you angry with her?
MARY: No.
TIM: I wish you didn't have to go back to work.
MARY: Me too, but you'll have your dad here.

As they move inside MARY*'s mobile phone rings.*

[*Into phone.*] Mary speaking … Raj. Thanks for calling back … Yep, the very same Mary Horton … Next week? That's perfect … Bye, bye.

TIM *re enters.*

TIM: Was that Dad?
MARY: No. Just an old work colleague.
TIM: I like you, Mary.
MARY: I like you too.
TIM: You know what, I think I like you more than anyone else.
MARY: What about your dad and Dee?
TIM: Nope. I can't help it. I just do. You're my Mary.

SCENE 21

Group home. Ten days later. Early July.

RAJ *is showing* MARY *through the group home.*

RAJ: There are nine group homes in this cluster. This one has five bedrooms—most do.
MARY: What made you give up the corporate life?
RAJ: Bored. Money isn't everything.
MARY: You were the brightest spark in the company.
RAJ: Corporate life wasn't for me.

MARY: Do you enjoy this work? Being a carer?
RAJ: Actually to be precise I'm a team leader. What can I say? It's frustratingly rewarding. You haven't changed a bit.
MARY: You need glasses. I'm practically dripping in grey hair.
RAJ: We have overnight support staff.
MARY: Good-sized garden. So five housemates.
RAJ: Technically they're called 'consumers'.
MARY: Consumers? Sounds like a commodity.
RAJ: Don't get me started. You still at the Manx Group?
MARY: I was headhunted by END-CORE.
RAJ: Not surprised.
MARY: Do any of the 'consumers' work?
RAJ: Three go to work and two go to a day program.
MARY: Interesting set-up. Do they all get along?
RAJ: We have the odd squabble. Occasional bust-up. Nothing serious.
MARY: Are they heavily medicated?
RAJ: None of your god-damned business.
MARY: Sorry, privacy.
RAJ: Yes, Ms Horton, privacy. Let's just say the pharmacy sends Christmas cards.

MARY takes in the view, and quietly contemplates the house.

So, who are you group home shopping for?
MARY: Oh yes, good point. A friend. Tim.
RAJ: How old is he?
MARY: In his mid-twenties.
RAJ: How do you know him?
MARY: He does some gardening around the house.
RAJ: What's his disability?
MARY: I'm not actually sure. He gets 'anxious' for want of a better word. Sometimes I forget he has one.
RAJ: Okay.
MARY: His dad wasn't keen for him to attend his mum's funeral.
RAJ: That's a shame.
MARY: Can't cope in crowds apparently.
RAJ: Did she pass away recently?
MARY: A couple of weeks ago.

RAJ: Right. Still raw.
MARY: If there was some type of emergency, say Ron couldn't look after him, do you offer 'consumers' temporary care?
RAJ: Respite. No. We don't. And now you'd be hard pressed to find a place that does.
MARY: Surely there's a demand?
RAJ: Massive. Doesn't quite fit the funding structure sadly. 'Code' for no profit in it.
MARY: You're kidding me.
RAJ: Oh I'm not. It's pretty absurd. You're caught between the devil and the deep blue sea. Organising long-term care can take years.
MARY: It all sounds very complicated.
RAJ: That's because it is.

SCENE 22

Mary's cottage. Early August.

RON *is talking to* DEE *via Zoom on Mary's laptop.*

DEE: Melbourne's a different pace than Sydney, I think it's the trams. But the people seem so much friendlier.
RON: How's Nate settling in?
DEE: Fine.
RON: He got any work prospects?
DEE: A couple. How's Tim?
RON: Very quiet. I'll give him a yell so he can say hello.
DEE: It's okay, Dad. How are you?
RON: It'll be a month tomorrow. I still can't fathom it.
DEE: Are you sleeping okay?
RON: Here and there.
DEE: I know this isn't a good time, but I've been thinking about putting some paperwork together for you.
RON: What sort of paperwork?
DEE: Enduring Power of Attorney. Guardianship.
RON: Right.
DEE: I feel like we're at the stage where it might be a good idea to at least consider it.
RON: For me or for Tim?

DEE: For both of you.

> MARY *enters with a cup of tea.*

RON: I'll go and find him.

> RON *exits.*

MARY: Hi.
DEE: Hi.
MARY: How are you both settling in?
DEE: Fine.
MARY: Good.
DEE: You don't need to fill the air. I'll happily wait in silence.
MARY: You are nothing if not honest.
DEE: Some call it blunt.
MARY: Fair enough.
DEE: I do need something from you though.
MARY: What's that?
DEE: A postal address. If Tim is going to spend so much time with you, I'd like to send him a mobile phone. I want to be able to talk to him whenever he wants.
MARY: Great idea. I can show him how to use it.
DEE: Thanks. I do have one other question that's burning on my lips.
MARY: Which is?
DEE: Are you fucking my brother?

> RON *enters, followed by* TIM.

RON: Here he is.
TIM: Hi, Dee.
DEE: How's my big brother?
TIM: I'm going swimming with Mary.
DEE: I miss you, Tim. Do you miss me?
TIM: No. Dad and I went fishing too.
DEE: Did you catch anything?
RON: A cold.
TIM: Come on, Mary.
MARY: When you've finished speaking to your sister.
DEE: I'd love you to visit, Tim.
TIM: But I'm going for a swim.

DEE: Not now, I meant in a couple of months.
TIM: No thanks. Come on, Mary.
DEE: Enjoy your swim.

> TIM *exits.*

RON: Good to see your face, love. Give my best to Nate.
DEE: Love you, Dad.
RON: Bye, love.

> MARY *closes the laptop, grabs her towel and goes to leave.*

Thanks, Mary. Do you think Tim would be okay if I head down to Sydney for a day? I've got an appointment with my solicitor.
MARY: Totally fine.
RON: I need to sign some papers and get some advice on the house too.
MARY: I'd be happy to be a sounding board, anytime.

> RON *looks out down to the beach at Tim.*

RON: I might take you up on that. He was hopeless at school. We probably should never have pulled him out. Tantrums were unbelievable. We never dreamt he'd have the patience to learn anything, let alone read … until you came along. All said and done though, Joy raised a good boy.
MARY: You both did.
RON: Mary, if anything ever happens to me, would you consider looking after Tim?

SCENE 23

Group home. Days later.

MARY: I just wish I could make this situation right.
RAJ: What's changed?
MARY: Ron. He's keen for me to take more responsibility over Tim.
RAJ: Is Tim back at the workshop?
MARY: He doesn't work in a workshop. He works for a builder.
RAJ: I just assumed—
MARY: No, he's not back at work. Not yet.
RAJ: He needs to be pushed back into his routine.
MARY: He's too withdrawn.

RAJ: My opinion, take it or leave it, is get him back to work. Keep him busy.
MARY: He needs time to grieve.
RAJ: He needs to get back to work. He needs routine.
MARY: God, you're harsh.
RAJ: Who taught me that?
MARY: Didn't think you ever listened.
RAJ: Who's he with now?
MARY: Ron.
RAJ: Get his sister onside. What's her take?
MARY: Not my biggest fan. She thinks I'm sleeping with Tim.
RAJ: What a mess.
MARY: It is a bit. I never meant to get so involved, but here I am.
RAJ: You want my honest advice?
MARY: Please.
RAJ: It's time to bite the bullet and kick them all out.
MARY: I can't.
RAJ: Party's over.
MARY: I'm racked with guilt.
RAJ: Racked with guilt? That's a departure from the take-no-prisoners boss I worked for.
MARY: There's got to be other solutions.
RAJ: If you want to push on, get him into the system. Get a doctor's referral for a social worker. They'll find a support coordinator who will investigate funding. He'll probably need an occupational therapist to assess him too.
MARY: Sounds like we're jumping on a merry-go-round.
RAJ: That's because you are. I've got to be straight with you, Mary, funding's tight and I just don't think Tim fits the bill. It's going to be tough.
MARY: I hear you.
RAJ: Do you? He's got three basic options—stay with his dad, supported living like a group home or a private rental. Do you want the quickest way out?
MARY: What's that?
RAJ: Set him up in a boarding house.
MARY: I've read horrendous stories about boarding houses.

RAJ: Probably all true. Have you talked to his dad yet?
MARY: No. It feels like such a tough conversation to have.
RAJ: Tough conversations used to be your forte.
MARY: This one's different.

SCENE 24

Mary's cottage. Four days later.

MARY *is reading documents.*

RON: I've been working on a plan. My will, insurance policies.
MARY: I thought Dee was having papers drawn up.
RON: I'm one step ahead of her.
MARY: She'll want Power of Attorney.
RON: She'll have it. Over me. But you'll have Power of Attorney over Tim.
MARY: She'll want that too.
RON: You and I both know Tim won't survive five minutes under their roof.

    MARY *picks up a pile of bank statements.*

MARY: There's literally tens of thousands in this account.
RON: And there's a term deposit somewhere in there too.
MARY: How did he manage to accumulate all this money?
RON: Every Friday he'd hand me his wages, and every Monday morning I'd bank it. Every last cent.
MARY: I just need time to consider the practicalities of taking this all on. It's just … my work. It's incredibly time-consuming. Have you talked to Dee about any of this?
RON: Not yet.
MARY: Ron, do you ever think much about Tim's life after—
RON: Me? I never used to, but now it keeps me awake at night. I'm worried sick.

    Silence.

Our biggest mistake was that we never planned ahead for him. If I was younger it'd be different. There's nothing left with Joy gone. I'm done.

> MARY *moves her chair closer and comforts* RON. *She becomes aware that* TIM *is watching them. He's filled with rage and runs off.*

What's wrong with him?
MARY: Stay here. I'll go after him.

SCENE 25

TIM *is squatting at the water's edge, rocking in anger.* MARY *enters.*

MARY: Tim?
TIM: Don't touch me.

> MARY *attempts to comfort him.*

Get away.
MARY: What's wrong?
TIM: I hate you.
MARY: Why?
TIM: You like Dad.
MARY: That doesn't mean I don't like you.
TIM: You're lying. You like him more.
MARY: What? Because I gave your dad a hug? He was upset. He's feeling really sad.
TIM: I'm feeling sad too.
MARY: I know, I know. Remember when we talked about what happens when people die? How they get too tired to go on? I think it's happening to your dad.

> TIM *begins to listen.*

I know you miss your mum, but it's different for your dad. He just wants to lay down next to your mum and be with her again. That's why I was hugging him. I know I've given him a lot of time but he has so little time left.
TIM: He wants to be with Mum?
MARY: He misses her so much.

> TIM *'burrows' into* MARY*'s lap.*

Your dad is a good man. He's devoted his life to you. Now it's our chance to give him back just a little of what he's given you. Could you maybe think about that?

TIM: I can think a little. But I know I'm not right.
MARY: Tim—
TIM: —I'm not. I'm not right. Not normal.
MARY: Don't say that.
TIM: But I'm not. I don't want to be like this. I'm not stupid. I'm not dumb. I'm not. I'm not.
MARY: No you're not. It's okay. Breathe. It's all okay.

He calms.

TIM: I want to be like you.
MARY: You are.
TIM: You're the only one who treats me like I'm not different.

TIM hugs her, holds her tight and presses his cheek against hers until he fumbles to her lips. MARY tries to resist. She pulls away again but TIM brings her closer.

MARY: Tim, don't.

He kisses her again, she tries to push her fingers against his lips, but succumbs and takes his hair in her hands as they kiss before MARY wrenches herself away from TIM.

God, that should never have happened.

TIM tries to kiss her again.

Tim. We can't do that.
TIM: Why not? It feels good.

He tries again.

MARY: No, no, no, Tim.
TIM: But I liked it. Didn't you?
MARY: Yes … no … I mean there are some things friends shouldn't do.
TIM: Wow, it felt fantastic. I'm tingling. Aren't you tingling?
MARY: Yes, but … if we kiss like that, it's hard for us to stay friends.
TIM: Why?
MARY: God knows I like you a lot, but I can't kiss you.
TIM: But it feels good.
MARY: You have to promise me something. Our kiss has to stay a secret.
TIM: Why?
MARY: Please don't tell your dad.

TIM: But—
MARY: Please. For your dad's sake. Just this one secret.
TIM: Okay. What you said about Dad? I get it. Is this why Dee was angry? The day you picked me up, Dee was yelling.
MARY: She was.
TIM: At you.
MARY: How could I forget?
TIM: Did she think we'd been kissing?
MARY: Something like that.

They return to the cottage.

SCENE 26

Front lawn of Mary's house. Late August.

TIM *is mowing the lawn.* MARY *appears with* RAJ.

MARY: Tim, have you got a minute?

TIM turns off the mower and takes off his noise-cancelling earmuffs.

I want to introduce you to Raj. We used to work together.
TIM: Hi, Raj.
RAJ: Great to meet you, mate. Garden looks great.
TIM: Yeah, we're getting there. Spring is nearly here. The flowers should be back in bloom soon.
RAJ: Sounds like you've put in a lot of hard work.
TIM: Thanks, it's paid off.
RAJ: Sure has.
TIM: Are you staying for tea, we're having fish and chips?
RAJ: No, mate, I've gotta head back to work.
TIM: Okay, I better finish the lawn.

TIM's mobile phone rings. TIM *answers it and slowly moves away.*

It's Dee. Hi … I was talking to Raj. He's Mary's friend.
RAJ: He's quite the handsome young man.
MARY: He is.
RAJ: I'm intrigued. What's the update?

MARY: Ron's convinced his sister won't want him.
RAJ: What do you want?
MARY: Ron's signed over Tim's affairs to me.
RAJ: And you don't want that?
MARY: She'll make my life hell, if something ever happens.
RAJ: Legally she can't.
MARY: She's a lawyer and she hates me.
RAJ: Got it. But you love a good legal stoush?
MARY: This is different. She's convinced I'm sleeping with Tim.
RAJ: Are you?
MARY: Raj!
RAJ: It's not a crime.
MARY: Something happened a couple of weeks ago. Tim got angry. He took off. I chased him. The long and the short is he kissed me.
RAJ: And?
MARY: Raj, he kissed me.
RAJ: Ah right, 'retards' can't have sex.
MARY: I didn't say that.
RAJ: What? You're not allowed to be intimate because he's a young and highly attractive, virile man?
MARY: Be serious.
RAJ: Mary, can I cut to the chase? In five minutes flat, I can tell you that man is not group-home material. But the writing is on the wall, isn't it? You'll dump him. His dad will cark it. He'll come into a shitload of cash and the sister won't give a rat's arse about him. Neither will the NDIS, because they won't even know he exists. And then he'll live out his days in a boarding house, a lonely, lost soul. What a fairy-tale ending.

   This is all too ridiculous for words.
MARY: What do you mean by that?
RAJ: There's clearly another solution staring you right in the face.
MARY: Tell me.
RAJ: Blind Freddy can see it.
MARY: See what?
RAJ: Just get married.
MARY: Don't be absurd.
RAJ: Think about it. You said the sister's going to make your life a misery.

MARY: It's guaranteed.
RAJ: Get married. She'll never find a court in the land that'll force you to divorce him.
MARY: She'd block it before it began.
RAJ: Don't invite her.
MARY: I can't marry someone who's—
RAJ: Half your intellect.
MARY: I'm no fit partner for him.
RAJ: You mean he's no fit partner for you.
MARY: No, I don't mean—
RAJ: Quit this self-sacrificing bullshit. It's no big deal.
MARY: Are you out of your mind?
RAJ: Clean your mirrors, Mary Horton. You are as attractive as the day I met you.
    Do you think he'll get bored with you?
MARY: No.
RAJ: Will you get bored with him?
MARY: Never.
RAJ: Then what's your problem?

SCENE 27

Evening.

MARY: I just don't know if I can do it.
EMILY: He's fallen head over heels in love with you.
MARY: I'm old enough to be his mother.
EMILY: I'm old enough to be his grandmother but I'd marry him in a heartbeat.
MARY: I'm no spring chicken.
EMILY: Well, whatever you think of yourself, he is clearly seeing someone very different.
MARY: Em, we are not talking ten years. We're not even talking twenty years.
EMILY: What does it matter? He wants to be with you.
MARY: I am twenty-nine years older than him. Twenty-nine.
EMILY: What are you worried about? Gossip? I hate to be the bearer of bad news, but you're getting that already. Give him a big 'tonguey'

in the middle of the roundabout—give the neighbours something to really talk about.

MARY: How will people treat him if we're together?

EMILY: You're together now. What's really going on, Mary?

MARY: I've never felt like this.

EMILY: Like what?

MARY: When he kissed me, I felt so … conflicted, so mortified.

EMILY: But?

MARY: I didn't want it to stop. I didn't want him to stop. My whole body shook like nothing before. It was magical. Like cracker night inside. Fireworks.

EMILY: There is absolutely no shame in that.

MARY: But, he's never been exposed to—

EMILY: Sex?

MARY: Every time he looks at me, he just wants to keep kissing me again.

EMILY: Half your luck.

MARY: There is one other tiny matter that's niggling at me too.

EMILY: Spill it.

MARY: I can't. It's embarrassing

EMILY: Try me.

MARY: I've never had an … you know.

EMILY: An? Oh!

MARY: It all feels so loaded.

EMILY: Well, the clitoris is a sensitive beast.

MARY: How will I know?

EMILY: Oh, it's fabulous. You'll feel like a quivering lioness. Your legs will shake with pleasure. It's like one big throbbing 'sneeze' out of your vagina.

MARY: A 'throbbing sneeze'?

EMILY: Was that too much?

MARY: A little.

EMILY: It's just about letting go. Discover it together. Hell, that's half the fun.

MARY: I never realised how much I've missed out on. Never loved anyone like this.

EMILY: Until now?

SCENE 28

The Melville home. A couple of days later.
RON *is sitting in his armchair.* MARY *is there.*

RON: You've changed your mind?
MARY: Tim and I have a pretty unique friendship, and he's become attached to me, Ron. I'd go so far as to say he loves me.
RON: Yes he does.
MARY: From the minute I met him, we had a connection. We're so different, but we complement each other. Am I making any sense?
RON: Completely.
MARY: I'd never given it much thought … not until your daughter gave me a rude awakening.
RON: She has that knack.
MARY: Ron, have you purposely kept Tim sheltered in terms of his sexuality?
RON: Truth be told, yes. In his teenage years everyone was after him—women and men. We kept a lid on it until he started work. I know his workmates torment the bejesus out of him. He's told me about the odd dirty movie, but they've never led him astray with women. Not to my knowledge, anyway.
MARY: It's hard to escape it these days. The reason I ask is that Tim decided to show me that he liked me.
RON: What'd he do?
MARY: He tried to kiss me.
RON: Jesus. I'll have a talk to him.
MARY: No need. We sorted it, but I have been seeking some advice and I wanted to share it with you. Ron, I'm in my fifties. God only knows what Tim sees in me.
RON: The advice?
MARY: A simple solution—emotionally, legally, practically—is that Tim and I could … get married.

    RON *remains expressionless.*

I know this probably comes as a bit of a shock. It did to me. I argued against it but it made me see Tim in a completely different light. I, rightly or wrongly, had him cast in my mind as not a whole person. I'd completely ignored the fact that Tim deserves to get as much out of life as anyone.

God only knows he could do so much better than me, but he loves me. He says as much every time I'm with him. And if I'm to be completely honest, I love him too. I'm in love with him. This is the very first time in my life I actually feel happy. He makes me feel safe. And he'll be safe with me.

Hopefully I'll live a long life and we'll have years ahead of us. I've been thinking about the alternative; to walk away and forget him. I can't bear that thought. I'd be miserable.

I've considered just living together, but if we were married, Dee couldn't swoop in and take him away … and once you're gone, she'd become his legal guardian. And, let's not beat around the bush, that'd be the end of me having any contact with him. I'd never cope with that. It'd break me.

Of course, if you object, I'll respect that and it'll be the end of it. But with all my heart, Ron, it just feels right. I love him. I want to marry him. If he'll have me.

RON: You're right about one thing. People might cope with you just living together but they'd see this marriage as wrong. You're a fine person, Mary. But so is Tim. You've been completely honest with me so I'm going to be completely honest with you.

RON *contemplates his response.*

I couldn't wish for a better life for my son. I'd be over the moon if you and Tim were to marry.

MARY: You mean that?
RON: I wouldn't say it if I didn't mean it, Mary.
MARY: Thank you. Thank you, Ron.
RON: I have just one request.
MARY: What's that?
RON: This marriage happens soon. If I'm there, it will leave no doubt in anyone's mind that you both have my blessing.
MARY: And Dee?
RON: I'll have the greatest of pleasure of informing her after the event.
MARY: Thank you, Ron … for everything.

RON: My pleasure. I do have one other question.
MARY: What's that?
RON: Have you asked Tim?

SCENE 29

Early morning. The next day.

As the music plays we see TIM *and* MARY *in deep discussion. He jumps up bursting with excitement.*

TIM: Let's get married today.
MARY: We have to go to work today. How about next Friday?
TIM: Yes.
MARY: Shall I ask Harry if you could have that day off?
TIM: Yes. I'm going to marry Mary! I'm going to marry Mary!
MARY: You better get ready for work. Harry will be here any minute.

> TIM *races inside.* MARY *calls over the fence to Emily.*

Emily! Em!

> EMILY *appears.*

EMILY: What's wrong?
MARY: Long story … have you got two minutes?
EMILY: For you, anything. What's up?

> *We hear the distinct sound of Harry's truck horn.*

MARY: Too late to explain.

> HARRY *appears.* JIM *tags along.*

HARRY: Morning, ladies. Timmy ready?
MARY: Nearly. Do you have a minute, Mr Markham?
HARRY: Harry. Sure.
MARY: Harry. Would it be possible for Tim to take a day off work next week?
HARRY: We're a bit flat chat, but I guess we could manage.
MARY: Good, because Tim and I are getting married next Friday.
HARRY: Bullshit.
JIM: Fuck me.
MARY: No thanks.

EMILY: Yahoo!
MARY: Can I ask, is Tim a good worker?
HARRY: He's bloody exceptional.
MARY: Then can I be frank? You and I both know Tim has been the brunt of sustained ridicule and harassment by your crew. Correct?
HARRY: Well, they don't mean any—
MARY: Don't fuck with me, Harry. I have an eye-witness.

> EMILY *waves, smiling broadly.*

And I suspect I'd find plenty more. I'll say this once. It all ends today. If Tim ever comes home with so much as a hint of harassment or intimidation, I will drag you in front of any court that'll listen. What is it, ten, twelve years without super, or holiday pay? I won't just break your business, Harry Markham, I will fucking destroy you. Do I make myself clear?
HARRY: Couldn't be clearer.

> TIM *appears.*

JIM: DT!
TIM: Sorry, Harry.
HARRY: All good, Timmy. Tim.
MARY: Great news, Tim. Harry's putting you on the books. And giving you a pay rise.
TIM: Wow. Thanks, Harry!
HARRY: Uh ... you're welcome.
MARY: Oh, and Harry, Tim will give you his account details.
HARRY: Thank you.
JIM: Come on, DT.
TIM: My name is Tim.
JIM: Come on, Tim.

> EMILY *waves to* HARRY *and* JIM *as they exit, before heading home.*

TIM: I'll see you tonight, Mary.
MARY: Yes, Tim, you will.

> TIM *exits.* MARY *exhales and looks at* EMILY.

EMILY: 'I will fucking destroy you'? Not exactly the language of a blushing bride.

SCENE 30

The first week of September.

We hear wedding music as the stage is transformed for a wedding.

TIM *and* MARY *are facing each other.*

MARY: I, Mary Elizabeth Horton, take you, Timothy Melville, to be my husband. I promise to spend the rest of my life earning your love, to show you the respect and honour you deserve and I'll try never to get cranky. I promise this, all the days of my life.

>TIM *takes a piece of paper from his pocket to read his vows.*

TIM: I, Timothy Melville, take you, Mary Elizabeth Horton, to be my wife. Every part of me now belongs to you and you belong to me. When I look into your eyes, I am the happiest man in the world. I promise to love you, to protect you, I promise to make you laugh, every day of my life.

>*They exchange rings. The lights change and we are in the cottage. The music continues.*

SCENE 31

Mary's cottage. Later in that evening.

Music continues as TIM *leads* MARY *to the cottage.*

TIM: Are you okay?

>MARY *nods.*

MARY: I'm more than okay.

>TIM *takes* MARY *by the hand. They walk through the cottage, turning out the lights.*

>*They make their way to the bedroom, in a silhouette of light.*

TIM: Am I allowed to kiss you now?

>*We witness the beginnings of their love-making. The lights slowly fade.*

SCENE 32

Cemetery. Dusk. Late October.

TIM *and* DEE *are standing by Ron's grave after the burial service.* DEE *is six months pregnant.* MARY *and* NATE *are standing nearby.*

TIM: Do you think he's with Mum?
DEE: They're together again, just like Dad wanted.
TIM: I still want to tell him so many things.
DEE: Me too, Tim.
TIM: Like how much I love living with Mary.
NATE: Come on, Timmy, let's go and check out some old gravestones.

>NATE *and* TIM *go for a walk through the cemetery, leaving* MARY *and* DEE.

MARY: I'm sorry for your loss.
DEE: I don't need your condolences.

>*Silence.*

I've read the will. I've got to hand it to you, you got exactly what you wanted. Possession is three-quarters of the law. And I'm not talking about the house.
MARY: Tim's happy. Aren't you pleased about that?
DEE: How do I know he's happy?
MARY: Visit us and see for yourself.
DEE: No thanks. But I want some assurance that he's okay.
MARY: How do you envisage that assurance taking place?
DEE: I want him to see someone, I don't know, a counsellor? I'm not sure yet.
MARY: Absolutely. I'll even cover the cost.
DEE: No. I'll cover the cost. And I want to see Tim whenever I'm in Sydney. Alone. No excuses.
MARY: Wouldn't have it any other way.
DEE: I guess the next time I see you will be at your funeral.
MARY: Bring your tap shoes.
DEE: I wouldn't want to wake you.

MARY *hands* DEE *an envelope.*

MARY: Here.

DEE: What's this?

MARY: Power of Attorney. Guardianship. My will. If anything happens to me, it's all here. It's all yours.

DEE *takes the envelope.*

DEE: I still don't like you.

MARY: You don't have to like me, but our common ground is Tim. We both love him and want the best for him. Am I right?

DEE: I'll just never understand any of this.

MARY: What's to understand? Nate is everything you're not but you chose each other. It's the same for Tim and I.

DEE: Not quite.

MARY: Have a safe trip back to Melbourne.

DEE *meets up with* NATE *and* TIM. *She hugs* TIM *in the distance and she and* NATE *exit.*

TIM *returns to* MARY.

God she reminds me of me.

TIM: Did you get cranky with each other?

MARY: No. Everything was fine.

TIM: I'll miss him.

MARY: So will I.

TIM: I liked him better than anyone in the world, except you, Mary. Bye, Dad.

MARY: Come on, Tim. Let's go home.

Blackout.

THE END